The Art of
PERCEPTION

How to 10x your business to make money faster and easier while fully protecting your assets

Albert Corey

Copyright © 2019 by Albert Corey

The Art of PERCEPTION

All rights reserved. No part of this publication may be reproduced, distributed, or transmitted in any form or by any means, including photocopying, recording, or other electronic or mechanical methods, without the prior written permission of the publisher, except in the case of brief quotations embodied in critical reviews and certain other noncommercial uses permitted by copyright law. For permission requests, write to the publisher, addressed "Attention: Permissions Coordinator," at info@beyondpublishing.net

Quantity sales special discounts are available on quantity purchases by corporations, associations, and others. For details, contact the publisher at the address above.

Orders by U.S. trade bookstores and wholesalers. Email info@BeyondPublishing.net

The Beyond Publishing Speakers Bureau can bring authors to your live event. For more information or to book an event contact the Beyond Publishing Speakers Bureau speak@BeyondPublishing.net

The Author can be reached directly BeyondPublishing.net/AuthorAlbertCorey

Manufactured and printed in the United States of America distributed globally by BeyondPublishing.net

New York | Los Angeles | London | Sydney

Hardcover ISBN: 978-1-949873-32-0

Table of Contents

Author's Welcome 5

Perception: An Introduction 7

Chapter 1: We All Start Somewhere 15

Chapter 2: Owning The Dream 23

About the Author 77

Author's Welcome

I don't know who is more thrilled with what you are about to read, me or you.

There is nothing that is more important to your and my personal success and our well-being than the notion of perception. Perhaps there is also nothing that is more misunderstood.

Most people I talk with believe perception to be the opposite of what it actually means. When I spoke with a friend recently about my book, he said, "Oh, you are going to teach people to lie." A business associate at church said something similar. "Perception? How can someone be successful not telling the truth?"

What? It's amazing so many do not understand the power of this beautiful word, perception.

Perception is the art of using the senses to understand something. It is a wonderful word, because it allows us to create a conversation with others, so that they might understand what truly is, rather than what isn't. Perception is communicating in the moment.

It is one of the most powerful truth-telling experiences known to man. Understood rightly, it forges strong relationships, creates satisfied clients, shapes reasonable expectations, and, most importantly, allows you to develop a healthy relationship with yourself.

Misused, the power of perception can destroy our lives. I am one of those guys who has grown up a little bit every day of my life. My great challenge has been to appreciate the person I am becoming and to communicate that emerging person to the people who are in my world. The perception others have of me and my business needs to be constantly evolving, in order to keep up with who I am becoming. In my world, paying attention to perception rules the day.

> *Perception is the art of using the senses to understand something.*

I am excited you have picked up this book. It means you are interested in how others think about you. It signals that you want to pay attention to the person you are becoming, rather than the person you used to be. It tells me that you are wanting those who matter most to have an accurate understanding of who and what you are. How others perceive us to be is, indeed, one of our most important goals in life.

We share that priority together.

Welcome to my world, the art of perception.

Perception: An Introduction

The Art of Perception is much more than a book that's going to teach you how you can make money. There are lots of books that can show you those tricks. Of course, it does do that, but that's not all.

It's also not just a book where I'm going to share the story of how I started my wonderfully successful accounting journey, despite my meager beginnings and no idea what I was doing. Of course, I will tell you that story, but this is much more.

The only reason you might consider picking up a book about perception would be if that book was going to deliver something special. *The Art of Perception* is a much bigger deal than my personal story and my thinking on how to build a thriving — and unconventional — accounting business. Perception is a massive idea, one that can be vital to anyone, no matter their background, industry, passions, dreams, desires, or goals.

Here is some truth up front. This book will absolutely be discussing certain strategies and systems I used in becoming a great accountant. I regularly make a seven-figure income. Come on, that's pretty good. But the truth is, *everything* I'm going to share with you can be applied to *any* kind of business, any life. All real success starts inside of our own gut.

What's fun is that these strategies are not coming to you from a lucky stiff who was born with a silver spoon in his mouth, gripping a Harvard diploma. Nope, it's coming from someone who has pulled himself up just about every slippery rung on the ladder of success. I have the bruises to show you. I come from a hard-working family of farmers in Lebanon. I never had any advantages handed to me. Not a single one. I was never allowed to take a shortcuts. I am old school. I earned and learned everything I ever got, including each and every life lesson.

Yes, I'm fully aware that this may not the best sales pitch for this book. It is the thinking of most people looking for success that their lessons and teachings should come from people who have lived a life of overwhelming wealth and success. Guess again. There are a lot of people who have had advantages along the way that most of us could only dream of. They are making a lot of money telling you and me how to do things they have never done themselves. You know the old saying, those who can't do, coach.

Would you rather take advice about success and perception from someone who had it all handed to them, or from someone who started at the bottom and knows all of the tips and tricks to make it to the top?

While it might embarrass some, I have no problem telling people that I just barely made it out of high school. I wasn't all that interested in people talking at me and could not wait to get out of school. And it was nothing short of a miracle that I not only got into, but also graduated college. I am still kind of shocked. No one ever accused me of being the best student, but I possessed the persistence and the drive needed to grind out success both in the classroom and afterward when school was behind me. I am really good at what I do, and my confidence in my ability to get the job done and done well is over the top. That is what made me different than many of my classmates, and why I am more successful than many of the people I went to school with (remember, I am now an accountant for a lot of them. I know what they make!).

When I graduated college, I stepped out into a world that didn't have many jobs to offer. Things were tight all over back then. I could have been picky. After all, I WAS A COLLEGE GRADUATE! I'M NOT DOING ANY OLD KIND OF JOB!

I could have moaned and griped about poor work options, weak pay, and lousy opportunities. But what good would that have done? I was hungry to work, eager to make a name for myself, and anxious to become a success. I wanted to shine. So, in those early years, I took whatever work I could get. I mean anything. It didn't matter to me how it might look on a resume. I was ready to grind.

I chose to work alongside my father in a tiny little hotel in South Florida as a housekeeper. Was it glamorous and fulfilling work? Hell no. I was cleaning rooms, picking up trash, and washing sinks and toilets. It was not the kind of job you were anxious to tell others about. It kind of screamed, LOSER. It was the job you picked up when no one would hire you. Not only that, but I wasn't even needed unless the people who had originally been hired to clean the rooms didn't show up. Wow. I was below the people who were at the bottom. I looked up at *everybody*. Crazy job for a college graduate with vision.

> *I was cleaning rooms, picking up trash, and washing sinks and toilets. It was not the kind of job you were anxious to tell others about. It kind of screamed, LOSER.*

There was a mission to my madness. When I started working in that hotel, I knew bigger things were coming. I knew that if I busted my ass, never gave up, and worked hard, something good was going to happen. And it did.

I got interested in accounting and eventually wound up starting my own tax preparation service in 1985. There was no internet way back then, no social media. If I was going to be successful in my new business, I was going to have to grind clients out of rocks. I would have to find clients the old-fashioned way. Wait a minute, I *was* the old-fashioned way, living in the old-fashioned world. I could not rely on social media to paint this beautifully branded picture of myself to the world. I had to do it by pounding the pavement and making calls. "Hello! My name is Albert Corey. I am an accountant. I can save you a lot of money."

I had to keep at it, knocking on doors over and over and over again. Even on the bad days, when no one responded or wanted to have a conversation with me about their taxes. Come on. Who wants to talk about their taxes? With bills piling up, don't think there were not a lot of times I thought about going back and cleaning rooms. At least *that* was money to buy food and pay the rent.

You will hear more about how I created success as we go along in our conversation. *The Art of Perception* is about you, about how you can accomplish your life goals. I can help you with that. Importantly, I will show you how to help people to perceive you as the successful person you know you can be and the successful person you deserve to be, despite the fact you might be cleaning motel rooms and taking out the trash.

The explosive truth we are discussing is as simple as this. The way others perceive you determines your chances for success. The opportunities for your success are shaped by how the world sees you. Success is a matter of perception.

Perception is fueled by how you understand yourself to be. The art of perception is about how the world understands you. I want to deepen your understanding of perception and how you can use it to your advantage. If you don't, you're going to get swallowed up by the circumstances of life. There are so many voices in the room wanting to define you and control your narrative that you need to become master of your perception in a way that makes you stand out from the crowd and celebrates your truth.

> *The way others perceive you determines your chances for success.*

While there are many different blueprints on how to manage perception, I'm going to share my own blueprint with you in the following pages. From floundering college grad cleaning dusty motel rooms to a successful accountant making more money than he had ever dreamed, I have earned the opportunity to be heard. I won't lie and say it was easy, but I will say it's more fun to be wildly successful than to scratch out a life day to day.

It requires some very practical steps. Give me your attention as I share what I learned in our conversation together. If you take that journey with me, I can promise you that your likelihood of success— no matter what your niche, market, or specialty— will increase significantly.

Keep your eyes on me. Look at me as an example. In the world of accounting, the market is beyond saturated. There is an accounting office on every corner. There are shifts in the way my business is done almost every year because of technology, economic factors, and rules and regulations. But I'm still here and thriving, successful long before the idea of going onto the Internet to file your own taxes was even a thought.

And I don't plan on going anywhere anytime soon. Why would I? I make seven figures a year and only work a hundred days each year. I travel when and where I want, and I have been fortunate enough to meet some of the most brilliant minds in the business world.

You can, too. It's right within your grasp.

You can wake up with that same confidence, and I want you to have it. Follow along as I show you how to master the art of perception.

Along the way, if you have questions, I'd be happy to serve as a mentor, even outside of the book. With more than thirty-five years of experience in the business development space, I am always willing and eager to meet new people, not only for the relationships, but to help them achieve their dreams and goals.

Don't believe me? I challenge you to go online and do a quick Google search for Albert Corey and see what others are saying. I have both the experience and the compassion to help others shape their own success, two things you don't often see at the same time in the same person.

Read on to see how you can get started on your own path to success and master the art of perception.

CHAPTER ONE

We All Start Somewhere

We live in a confusing world, where many people are out to make a quick buck. They love to hear stories about people who have become an overnight success. But we also live in a gritty world where some have come to understand the truth inside the raw rags-to-riches stories.

Let me say up front that you'll be getting something a little different from all that in this book.

I came from a very meager background. My father was an apple and olive farmer in Lebanon, and my mother was barely able to pay the bills, scraping together whatever she could to make ends meet. Needless to say, I was not born into money or instant fame. Nothing was ever given to me or to my parents.

My parents met after my father moved away from Lebanon. In search of a better life, he traveled to Australia before ending up in America. He made this journey with very little money and a single suitcase. Somewhere along the line, he met my mother. They fell in love, got married, moved to Florida, and I came along soon after.

I learned what it meant live inside the struggle early on. As I said, my mother was living a life that is described as paycheck-to-paycheck. We always did without, but I rarely noticed. She and my father worked at a little fruit stand that was owned by my mother's parents. Well, it was a fruit stand when the produce was in season. During the winter season, it became a stand to sell Christmas trees. In the spring, they'd sell Easter-themed plants. Mom also worked on the side as a hairdresser, doing anything she could to bring home some extra income for her growing family.

I attended school in the Miami area. I'd like to say this is the part of the story where I really start to shine and my story takes a great turn, but it doesn't. I wasn't a great student, pretty pitiful actually. I never really learned to read or write very well (WHAT! I am writing a book? Do miracles never cease?). I was constantly picked on by other kids and had trouble making friends. Luckily for me, this was in the 70s, and the educational bar was much lower than today. Few schools back then were concerned about test scores, and it was okay to be average, or a little bit below. You basically only needed to show up to class and have a good attitude to receive a passing grade.

If there was one single moment during my school years that would predict the sort of person I'd later become, it occurred in a middle school math class. I may not have been the best student, but I was curious to a fault. On one occasion, I was kicked out of math class and asked to stand in the hall for asking too many questions. Looking back on it, this might be one of the reasons I was relentlessly picked on. I had more questions than answers and drove everyone bonkers, adults and kids alike. Of course, I was a goofy-looking geek, too. That was probably the biggest reason.

I managed to make it through school and eventually enrolled in college at the University of South Florida. Similar to my previous classroom experiences, I wasn't the best student, but I managed to make the grades and eventually graduate. With my diploma, I entered a world that had very very little interest in a guy like me. I decided to go to work for my parents, a huge decision. By that time, their little fruit stand was a thing of the past. They were working at a motel, a cleaning business my father had purchased from my grandfather. The odds are, if you stayed at a motel in the Miami area between 1982 and 1990, there's a good chance I cleaned your room at some point and emptied your trash.

My parents had a few quirky thoughts about paying someone to work. They didn't like it, which was unfortunate for a college graduate like me trying to get ahead in the world. Some of that Aramaic culture left my father with an unusual sense of money. When it came to a paycheck for me, there really wasn't one. That's right, the wise guy college man got a job cleaning motel rooms and never received a paycheck. The thinking was, while I never truly got paid, everything I needed was paid for. I may have gone weeks at a time with no cash, but if something came up and I needed money, I would be allowed to just take it "off the top" from the motel revenue. It was a ridiculous way to live, and it was hard to figure out where it might all lead.

That's why I was in such a state of shock one day when my mother handed me my first tax return and I learned that I owed $192. WHAT? There had been no W-2 or other paperwork of any kind, but there I was, owing $192. I was speechless. I didn't even remember making $192 the entire year.

It was an important life moment for me. I was so taken aback by this unexpected news that I felt I needed to do something. It wasn't that I owed the money (well, maybe a little), but the fact I was sending the government money I had worked so hard to make when I made so little. It made me bristle. It made me want to know more about how this whole tax system worked, and if I could figure it out to help myself save money.

By the way, I love this country. There is never a second in any day I am not overwhelmed by the opportunity it offers each and every one of us. I love the fact that we have wonderful roads and bridges, clean water and toilets that flush, garbage that gets picked up every Tuesday, stoplights, schools, airplanes, and ten different kinds of potato chips. I love the diversity of people living together in healthy and loving communities. I really like this place. I just would like to not pay any more than I need to for the right to live here. Taxes are my ticket to the show. I prefer matinee prices.

In 1985, I decided to enroll in an H&R Block class. Talk about surprising everyone and changing the perception of who I was. Absolutely nobody saw that coming, least of all, me. I had made such a big deal about never walking back into a classroom again after I graduated college. People laughed and made fun of me. Deliberately going back to school? No one expected much to come of it.

My perception of myself was about to change. I learned so much my head blew up. Since I never was a fan of the educational experience, I assumed I had limits on my ability to learn in the classroom. Boy, was I wrong. Everything I heard made sense and stuck with me. I soaked it all in.

I remember one moment, in particular, to this day. I accompanied an accountant out to a client's house to work up a return for a $500 fee. My brain was going crazy. I was only making $4 an hour. Buzzers and lightbulbs started going off and flashing in my head. Five hundred dollars for a single return, are you kidding me? I had never seen someone make so much money for being an expert in something. I knew I could do this. It was life-changing.

I returned home that night and had a serious conversation with my Dad. I told him what I was learning and about one accountant doing a single return for $500. "I have to get in on that!" I remember telling my dad. "This is a big deal!"

My enthusiasm was met with a sneer. "Who the hell is going to come to you to get their taxes done? Gimme a break."

Encouraging, right? That's what happens when those closest to you are trapped by their perception of you. My dad never saw me successful in anything that really mattered. Why would

I be successful now? Who would trust someone who didn't have money of his own with resources that took a lifetime to accumulate? Easy answer. They wouldn't.

Perception was key. Sorry, Albert. Not you, not now, not ever.

It hurt. And it was confusing. Who was I really, the loser young man my dad saw me to be or the dreamer of dreams I felt myself to be? You and I have shared this moment with others in our lives many times. We are caught between the reality of what has been and the possibilities of what might be. It was the moment I began to understand how important perception is in using the senses to understand something. I wanted to appreciate who I was, what I was becoming, and how I wanted others to understand me. I wanted others to encourage my possibilities because they believed in me, not shoot me down because they had never seen this version of me. I would need to advance perception to an art form.

There was nothing I could really say to my dad. I would use his words as fuel to ignite my determination. I also knew that, looking backwards, he was partially right. No one in their right mind would come to THAT guy— a no-name, know-nothing individual— to get their important taxes done. Not the guy cleaning toilets in motel rooms. That important role of financial adviser was reserved for the best and the brightest and most trustworthy among us. I needed to figure out how to become that guy.

With the wind of my father's comments filling the sails of my imagination, I went to work with what I had and did the only thing that I could. I created Corey & Associates.

Who was I, the loser young man my dad saw me to be, or the dreamer of dreams I felt myself to be?

CHAPTER TWO

Owning The Dream

"Associates? Where did the 'associates' come from?" you might ask. And you wouldn't be the only one. It was a question I got a lot from people who knew me as they heard about my new business. "You have associates now? How? You were cleaning motel rooms last month. How did that all happen?"

In truth, my "associates" consisted of my mother answering the phones and my father making copies. I knew that clients considering using my accounting services would have more confidence in my work and commitment to excellent service if they knew I had others on my team.

My dad barely made my associate cut. He mostly grumbled and bitched about working with me the entire time. Not a big fan.

It wasn't long before my accounting business got busy. Something cool was going on, and people trusted me. I was working with a pencil (pause here for laughter), and I knew filling out returns by hand was going to limit my opportunity for success. If I wanted to grow the business, I needed to find some faster way to churn them out. Faster work meant more clients, which meant more revenue. After a few short months, I entered the space race, and in the summer of 1985, I purchased a Zenith computer. It cost me $5,000, my total take-home income from the year before. In 2019 dollars, that calculates to $11,902.56. You better know I believed in myself. Those looking to understand me had another data point in their shifting perception of me. I was breaking out, and others would have to work to keep up.

Have you noticed those who know you best sometimes are your greatest roadblocks to success? They rarely champion your efforts to grow and evolve and remind you of your past failures. Their perception of you is defined by old stories. Take no risks. You will only fall short again.

To say my father lost his mind is an understatement. He couldn't believe I had just spent more money than I had made the entire year before on a computer. The funny thing was, I had absolutely no idea how to use the thing. It was not user friendly in any way. It sat on my desk out of the box, and I stared at it. This was going to be interesting.

Dad called me screaming when he heard what I had done. He hung up in the middle of a sentence, jumped into his car, and drove over, so he could yell in my face. He wanted to see "the stupidest thing I had ever done." I was cursed out in both English and Aramaic. He may have made up a few new words, too. Yikes.

To be honest, he was right to be upset. In 1985, no one else was doing taxes with a computer. Personal computers were just becoming a thing and were difficult to figure out. There weren't accounting applications and easy-to-use programs like there are today. He couldn't understand why I would risk a good thing with an expensive computer I could hardly use. The user manual looked like flight simulations for a 747. It would bankrupt me.

The biggest question of all was how my business would react to such a thing. How could I know a client would even like having taxes calculated by an impersonal piece of machinery? How would the numbers get checked? And how could a computer keep up with the tax changes every year?

Okay, maybe I didn't think it through clearly. But somebody had to be first, otherwise nothing gets advanced. If I was afraid to fail, I would never succeed at anything great. I won't go so far as to say I was a pioneer, but look around now. Because a few of us pulled computers into our accounting businesses, we changed the entire body of work. That's pretty cool. Sorry, dad.

> *If I was afraid to fail, I would never succeed at anything great.*

The computer took some getting used to. We had to figure everything out, which meant we were figuring it out as we went along. There were no computer manuals on accounting. Nobody was doing what we wanted to do. I found some people who understood what computers were capable of, but they didn't understand accounting. I talked to people who were crackerjack accountants who had no idea of what a computer was. By the beginning of tax season, I knew enough to use my Zenith computer to push out some of our tax returns. My aggressive business strategy was reflected in the growth of my company. Clients loved me and thought I was a hoot. They loved being on the cutting edge and felt that computers were smarter than people, so how could it not good!

The investment in myself and my work had paid off in gold stars. I looked to take more risks in the next few years that kept me in front of the accounting industry. The perception of me and my business had not only changed, buy change became my middle name. A few years later, I purchased $3,000 worth of beepers and pagers. I was king of the hill, and nobody was going to push me off.

My father?

Through all of his clucking, I watched him change his perception of me and what I was capable of. Old stories were replaced with new stories, with new data and different outcomes. He began to think differently about the boy he had raised and the young man who cleaned motel rooms. I would do anything to be the best. I was always moving, always driving and always dreaming. I was the guy behind the eight-ball.

His perception of me changed in regards to my aggressive behavior. I saw risks as opportunities to excel while disrupting expectations. I sold those beepers and pagers out of a comic book store while I was pushing tax returns out the back of the shop. We were easy to find, because no business in the area had a name like mine.

Cards, Comics, and Taxes

You got it right. I was doing taxes in the same shop where I was selling copies of bestselling issue, "The Death of Superman". I was moving pagers and phone accessories under the same roof I'd prepare your tax returns. I was hot, I was different, and my clients got me. They loved me and loved my work and could read a comic while waiting to see me. I had shaped their perception of me to deliver their taxes excellently, on time, and at a fair price.

The business was going crazy. I was happy and pretty satisfied. I was supporting my three children and paying my bills and saving money for the first time in my life. I was completing more than a thousand returns each year. That is a massive amount for a single location. But there was still something missing, and I could not put my finger on it.

One day, a random customer walked into the store, a day that is as clear in my mind as yesterday. The client was flabbergasted that I would manage taxes in the same location where I sold baseball cards, Pokémon, and comics. "Man, this won't work. No way. I can't get my taxes done in a place like this." He left.

He wasn't being mean-spirited or demeaning. He was telling me how he felt, and it mattered to me. As I watched him walk away through the window, a switch flipped in my head. I knew I needed to evolve my thinking once again. Not everybody was going to like my goofiness. If I wanted to enlarge my client base and get even bigger, I needed to get my head clear on what these potential clients needed to know about me and the way I ran my accounting business. Once again, I needed to take control of the perception others had of me and my business.

I made major changes overnight. I moved $20,000 worth of phone accessories into the garage. I sold hundreds of comics for pennies to get them off the floor. I changed my store in a couple of weeks, deciding to focus solely on the tax side of things. I understood what I wanted people to think about working with me and the confidence I wanted to inspire, and I set out to make it happen.

PERSONAL NOTE

It's fun explaining to you the thinking behind building from scratch one of the most successful accounting practices in Florida. There were moments along the way that were not so fun. I left out the parts where I failed out of law school. Twice. I did not tell you I got kicked out of H&R Block. Twice. I didn't leave those moments out because of embarrassment, but because they were simply obstacles in my path to success. Your path to success is lined with challenges that may cause you to doubt yourself.

Never doubt. It is a true saying, what does not kill you makes you stronger.

No one wants to be understood as a failure. No one wants to be seen as incompetent. There is some failure in every story. The art of perception informs you how to be transparent with your truth. Thoughtful storytelling, the key to the art of perception, allows the entire truth to be told.

I think back to that younger version of me that got booted out of math class for asking too many questions. I felt like a failure standing alone in the hallway. I remember a teacher walking by and wisecracking something about me not being able to keep my mouth closed long enough to sit through an entire class without getting thrown out. Man, that really hurt, and I battled the temptation of thinking like a loser.

Being invited to remove myself from the classroom wasn't a failure at all (let the record show, I still got an A in the class). But wow, the feeling of isolation from my classmates and being outed as a troublemaker and distraction stuck with me. I didn't appreciate that feeling then, and I don't appreciate it now. It eventually drove me to become successful in my field, taking risks and refusing to give up on anything. Send me to stand out in the hall for asking questions? I'll show those bastards.

It's all about perception, even right down to the smallest of details.

I'll share the ending to my story later in this book. First, let's talk about how to communicate the best possible version of you imaginable!

THINKING
What to Think About the Things that Matter

The way we think about things is pretty important. It shapes the way we do what we do. Our values and priorities and the lists of things we will do today all come from what we think about things. I know it sounds simple, but it's true. Change the way someone thinks, and you change the way they live their life.

First Thing to Think About
If you want to be successful, you have to want it. There is no substitute for the fire in the belly. Everyone is passionate about something. For one, it may be to make a new friend. For another, to solve a problem. Yet another, to perform.

Some of us have a passion to be successful. It is a gift, like playing the piano. Not everyone has been designed to do all the little things it takes to be successful, just like not everyone has been designed to do all the work day after day, year after year to become a prima ballerina.

It's all about the fire. Even in our most sacred of journeys, it's about our passion. The most repeated verse in the Bible is found in the Old Testament. Almost one hundred times, God is heard saying the exact same phrase, "If you seek me, I will let you find me." Wow. The fire in the belly is what determines our ability to find our way to what we want. Even to God.

It's true that success means different things to different people, depending on the gift. Some want to be a success at influencing people. Others want the success of financial reward. Some want the success of growing things. Others want the success of turning a disaster into a success. It all depends on the gift.

Let's agree that success is not for everyone. If you don't have the gift and it doesn't get you excited, that's cool. Other things get your fire burning, and that's great. Find me, and I will give you money back for the book.

But if this book is in your hands, and you are looking for the way forward, and you want to be a rock star or make a difference or influence people or reach the highest mountain and success is the most important thing in your life, well, then maybe we are a match.

Here is our first thing to think about. Being the best at success is what you do.

> *Being the best at success is what you do.*

Success takes practice, like anything else. Hours and hours of practice. In sports, it is called repetition. Reps. Doing the same thing over and over and over and over and over and over and over thousands and thousands of times, until the little things, the mechanics of a motion, become automatic. Success is no different.

There are lots of lessons you need to learn, lots of small things to practice until they become automatic. Along the way, you will get bopped by a ball bouncing off your head, but that's okay. Catch the next one, and learn from the bruise. If you are going to achieve your goal of being successful, it will take some hard work to get there. Your God-given passion to become successful will give you the energy to keep coming back for more.

Let's talk about how to think about your path to success and how mastering the art of perception will make it a reality sooner than you might expect.

1 - DETERMINE TO MAKE YOUR SUCCESS A REALITY

You might as well get used to what's ahead for you. There is no job description or clock to punch. No user's manual for success. No truck to drive across the country with a paycheck waiting for you at the other side.

The journey to success is a part of success, itself. Like the hours of practice on the saxophone or throwing a ball against a wall, you want to embrace success as your thing, more than a thought or a dream you have. Like an athlete or creative talent, you are going to sacrifice time and energy to be the best at success. You will spend some money, like musicians do for the best instruments or ballplayers do to get the best glove on their hands. Being the best at success requires the best tools money can buy.

Success is more than a conference with star-studded speakers or a subscription to a video blog. It must become a part of your thinking, part of your life today. It is your reality. I was a success when I was cleaning motel rooms and emptying trash. I was on my journey. It was in my head. Like a musician born a musician, I was born successful. I needed to become masterful at what I had in my heart to do. It's true for you. Success is your reality. You are just getting better at it.

It's scary to think that way if you have been told you aren't good enough. For some, just looking in the mirror tells you success may not be in the cards. Take a look at me standing next to Tony Robbins. Come on, really. No one is going to place any bets on the short guy.

You and I work on our success every day. We plan and schedule our time to make ourselves a little better with each passing moment. As we plan, we are living out the life of a successful person, and it becomes easier to know our success as a reality. Being the best at success is what we are all about.

2 - LEARNING FROM THE BEST - THE 21ST CENTURY ADVANTAGE

I call it 'the 21st century advantage'. You are a screen away from learning from the best in any field you can imagine. THERE ARE NO SECRETS ANYMORE! Anyone who is selling you a secret for a lot of money is a liar. Great thinking is out there at the push of a button, and rarely does it need to cost you as much as your cup of Starbucks.

We are always admiring the person who is better at doing what we love to do. If we are born to be successful, we find ourselves admiring those who have achieved success. "Man, I wish I could be as successful and as influential as that person."

You will need to evolve your perception of yourself to being as successful as those you seek to learn from. You have to see yourself as equal to or even greater than whoever it is you choose to follow. There's no advantage to thinking of yourself as small-time or the new kid on the block. You take your first step towards success with the mindset that you can swim in the same currents as the biggest fish in your pool.

Find that model or company and start studying them. Think like them. As you plan, ask yourself what they would do in any given situation or moment. If you want to emulate the most successful names or brands, you must approach your work like they do. You must think like they do. You must continue to enlarge your perception of what is possible, which happens to also be what is real.

What if you are just beginning to embrace being the best at success and changing your perception about what is true about you? What if you already maxed out your first credit card, just to get your enterprise off the ground, and you are flat broke?

None of that should stop you. Come on. Look at me. I had no money, and my head was in a toilet scrubbing out the grime, and there never was a moment I was more successful, because I understood who I was. MY PERCEPTION OF MYSELF WAS NOT DEPENDENT ON OUTWARD CIRCUMSTANCES. You have to think of yourself as just five minutes behind the most successful person you know.

You have to get the perception of who you are locked in.

Want to a successful tax preparer? Say out loud, "I'm just like H&R Block."

Want to be a best-selling author? Say out loud, "Stephen King and James Patterson better watch out."

It is only once you can say it about yourself and believe it that others will begin to believe it, too.

MY PERCEPTION OF MYSELF WAS NOT DEPENDENT ON CIRCUMSTANCES. You have to think of yourself as just five minutes behind the most successful person you know.

---

3 - GO BIG OR GO HOME

"Go big or go home" is a motto that just won't go away. It continues to express the passion of being all in and holding nothing back. Sports, business, the arts— all use it to express the fire in the belly, and leaving it all on the field. It's perhaps truest of all when it comes to evolving your perception of yourself. Being the best at success demands every ounce of you who are.

It's important that others understand this is your core truth, and that the perception people have of you is you will do whatever it takes to reach your goal. If you see yourself as small, insignificant, and inexperienced, those you are trying to influence and impress are going to see you the same way. As you think your way to success, repeat this simple truth about yourself all day long, "I go big."

Why think small? Why would you waste your time with any endeavor if you keep it contained to small goals, dreams, or visions? If you want people to perceive you as a powerhouse in whatever industry you are in, you must go big in all things.

Always think of yourself as a powerful and hungry dreamcatcher, looking for the next best way to grow your business and improve your brand. You'll be amazed at how quickly your oath to success changes when others start to see you in this light.

ACTION
Always Think Forward

A musician with a natural gift is required to hone his talent. There are no shortcuts to being the best. No matter how amazing and successful someone might seem, understand that their success was built from their commitment to both their gift and where they wanted that gift to take them. In the pursuit of their dream, they all had to learn, adapt, practice, get better, and make a pile of mistakes along the way. Some of them had to spend a few years making beds in motel rooms. You never know.

At some point, Bruce Lee had to throw his first untrained punch as a kung-fu novice.

At some point, Gordon Ramsay picked up his first frying pan and had no idea what to do with it.

At some point, Michael Jackson babbled his first song while he was playing with his toy trucks.

At some point, Tom Brady's unpracticed little hands weren't big enough to hold a football, much less throw it.

At some point, Mark Cuban likely shoved his first one-dollar bill from a lemonade stand into a piggy bank, without understanding anything about finance.

Get it? Setting your focus to obtaining success is pivotal, but it also requires drive and action for the long journey to success in order to be the best. It takes dedication and big steps forward.

You can take little, tiny baby steps if you like. The problem is that you will die before you get there if you are not trampled by someone hungrier first.

I am going to give you a few things to think about that will keep your days fresh and vibrant for your lifetime journey to be the best at success.

1 - BABY STEPS ARE FOR BABIES

There's nothing wrong with barely dipping your toes in the water or making baby steps. The reality is that time is the one commodity I cannot get you more of. It's a bitch. Forget running out of money.

You are running out of time.

Of course, one needs to be mindful of decisions and strategies that are required from day to day, especially when venturing into unknown endeavors. Come on. I spent a year of wages on a computer at a time no understood what a computer would do for my business. But if you have the capacity and the ability to make large strides and big steps, do it. I may not have been the smartest guy around, but I was intentional and mindful of my choices. Even as a young man, I knew I was running out of time. I could feel it.

Your pace, how fast you move and make choices, how fast you recover from a setback, how long you need to process information are all things others notice about you. And it matters to them. The perception about how you value and regard time is a matter of perception, because it is something true to understand about you. It makes a difference in your ability to be the best at success.

When you make decisions thoughtfully and quickly, you create big waves, and people notice. They make room for you in their life. If you make enough decisions, people will start to see you as a person in control of your life purpose who is growing and learning. You want them to perceive that about you. It is a good thing. It means that if they decide to intersect their life orbit with yours, chances are it will be a smooth relationship.

Your pace, how fast you move and make choices, how fast you recover from a setback, how long you need to process information are all things others notice about you. And it matters to them.

Remember the last time you took a road trip? A map might tell you the most efficient way to get there, and the trip will take six hours. But if you know another route that only takes four hours, wouldn't you take that, instead? Sure, you need to know the roads and have a familiarity with the area first. And that is no different than working towards success. There may be a pre-mapped route for you, and you can get there going the defined speed limit with all of the carefully plotted turns. But if you know another way, a way made shorter by taking a faster route, wouldn't you take that, instead?

Sometimes, taking larger than baby steps and speeding up means spending a little money. Might be. Get used to it. The path to being the best at success consists of taking risks. Success very rarely comes for free. It takes hard work and, very often, some extra dollars. Of course, you want them all to be smart spends, but you never really know until later— sometimes much later. Most of my best opportunities have come from expenditures that didn't work out quite like I anticipated. But if your perception of yourself includes a future in which your goals have been reached and you are making more money that you could have ever dreamed of, a few stray credit card bills here and there are more than worth it.

2 - HATERS GONNA HATE

Envy and jealousy have been basic human reactions since we were children. No one likes to be controlled by either of those emotions. They are built into the very nature of who we are. Of course, most often, it's up to us as to how we handle these feelings.

Some have a challenge with these emotions because of past life circumstances, or the chemical reactions inside of their bodies put them at a disadvantage. If you are reading this and often feel you have little or no control over how you are feeling, please don't be discouraged. You are not alone, and there are many wonderful doctors and therapists who can help you. Don't hesitate to call them.

Unfortunately, there are a lot of people who, by their own choice, tear others down when they become jealous or feel threatened. They like the way it feels, and it sucks for us. Some of them may be our closest friends or family members. That's a double suck.

As you climb your ladder of success, you're pretty much guaranteed to come across naysayers or people who simply can't handle your forward thinking. They'll question your methods and motives. They'll call you a fluke or any other number of names. Your first reaction to them will probably be to think something like, "Well, damn, what did I do wrong? Maybe I can't do this like I thought."

Forget about them. All of them.

Rarely do the people closest to you see how successful you are actually becoming. You are doing so many things right, both small and large, that those outside of your bubble of social influence won't be able to understand it. They become frightened by your desire to grow and get bigger and your desire to make yourself better. Frightened and critical and threatened. Their perception of you is not who you are becoming, but what you used to be. "Hey! Didn't you used to clean rooms at that motel?" You bet I did, friend. No one did it better.

Sometimes it's really hard not to listen to them. Maybe they know something about you that you don't see. It's one of the most common setbacks you'll face as you get closer and closer to success, to lose yourself in the constant questioning of your potential to be good. And you can count on those beauties in your fan gallery.

Setbacks are sometimes what your naysayers will use as ammunition against you. Even if the setbacks are the result of how these unbelievers perceive you, you can't let any of it slow you down. Even in the midst of troubles and obstacles, you must be forging ahead. If you stop long enough to consider the ill thoughts of others, you're going to grow stagnant and get stuck.

When possible, learn from your mistakes and setbacks. But you can move forward while you learn. Progress keeps your thoughts and motivation in a constant state of freshness—new ideas, new goals, and, if you're doing it right, a constantly evolving positive public perception of yourself and your work.

3 - MENTORS ARE THE KEY TO EXCELLENCE

Enough talk about negative influences. They'll come and go, and if you keep your eyes constantly forward, they usually end up being nothing more than a minor nuisance, like worrisome gnats around your head on a hot day.

Instead of focusing on the negative influences, you should be more worried about the positive influences you allow on the rungs of your ladder to success. Believe it or not, this does not always have to be someone you know well. Sometimes, it doesn't even have to be a figure in the same industry or niche you are in.

For argument's sake, let's say you're reading this book almost as a guideline of sorts. Because the words and wisdom are coming from me, you could view me as a mentor (a title I'd be honored to have!). The blueprint I am providing is not just guesswork; it has come through trial and error, and I know that they work, because my life is proof of it.

A good mentor should have that same level of success. It should be someone you can look up to and trust. It should be someone who seems happy to help. They may not always be outgoing or a "people person", but that doesn't matter. If they are willing to share advice and help you along the way and you can look at their life and see it as a measure of success, you've found a mentor.

Some people also think of mentors as coaches. People actually make careers out of being a so-called "life coach" these days. This is an empty term for the most part. A "coach" to help you along the way should be just like a coach for a sports team. They need to know the game (or your profession, or, at the very least, your end-goal) inside and out. They need to know the field, the rules, and what it takes to win.

If you can surround yourself with people like these, rather than those jealous naysayers we talked about above, you're setting yourself up for success.

4 - NEVER BURN A BRIDGE. EVER. NEVER.

Unless you absolutely can't get around it, never burn bridges with people you meet along the way. This includes people you bring along that end up under-performing or even flat-out failing you. Sometimes, you may come across people who seem to be trying to take advantage of you or even stealing your money. It might seem wise to just cut ties with these people and run, but nothing could be further from the truth.

Whenever it is possible, try to maintain friendships with everyone you meet. When a friendship just isn't in the cards, try to at least maintain a professional working relationship. This might seem counterintuitive to some people, but you have to always be thinking about the future...always moving forward.

That means keeping as many open relationships as you can. You never know when you might need someone again. If you don't see yourself needing that particular person or their talents (no matter how flimsy they may be), you may need their resources of contacts.

This is a pretty standard rule in just about any industry. The more people you have that you can go to for assistance, resources, or partnerships in the future, the more avenues to success you have.

Also, it goes without saying that when you burn a bridge with someone, it creates negativity. It allows that person the opportunity to take your name and livelihood out into the public eye and dirty it up. In terms of perception, you don't want anyone talking bad about you. And when you purposely burn bridges, you're inviting someone to do that very thing.

You never know when a point in the future will arise when you need to get from Point A to Point B, and there's a large chasm between the two. Without a bridge to cross to get there, you risk falling, failing, and letting the public see it happen.

CORPORATIONS AND BIG BROTHER
Casting a Big Shadow

Let's not only address the elephant in the room, let's move that sucker right out of here.

Yes, we live in a time where the term "corporation" might make most consumers cringe. When ruthless companies like Amazon are being blamed for killing small business and Disney is seen as a power-hungry media conglomerate that simply won't stop gobbling up entertainment properties, many people see corporations as evil.

But here's the thing…Amazon and Disney are essentially juggernauts now. That's because they started as something unique, always looked ahead and took massive actions to get where they currently are, and are always growing. Disney and Amazon are household names…so much so that while some might bemoan their size and influence, those same people still go to Disney movies or visit Disneyland. Those same people still order countless items from Amazon.

Why?

Because they are both valued and well-trusted names. Besides, not all corporations are seen as monstrous entities set on ruling the world. Oftentimes, when people see that your business is a corporation, it instills a sense of trust in them. Let's say you're running a small up-and-coming print shop out of your garage. It's just you, two friends, and a few pieces of equipment. Sure, there's a charm to being a small-town start-up. It's quaint and cheerful, and everyone loves a hopeful story of a business starting out.

But who do you think would have a bigger reach? Which company do you think will cast a bigger shadow over their industry? That company resting happily on the laurels of being a small-time print shop, or a shop that presents itself as a corporation? Who do you think is going to get more work? Who do you think the typical consumer is going to be more willing to trust with their time and money?

That's right; time and time again, the corporation is going to get that customer. Whether we like to admit it or not, the consumer mindset is basically trained to trust larger entities when it comes to their hard-earned money.

But it's more than just perception. Running your business as a corporation opens you up to other benefits as well.

1 - PROTECT WHAT'S YOURS, THE VALUE OF ASSET MANAGEMENT

Let's just face facts. Not every business succeeds. Sometimes, it takes a series of failures to lead to that first huge success. Because of this, asset protection and liability is very important, should the business go south. By filing as a corporation, you are essentially setting up an impenetrable wall around your company and all of its assets. No matter why the business might go under, being a corporation protects you from getting sued or losing additional money or resources.

Let me give you a real-world example of this. Let's say Billy is running his own painting business. After a couple of years, he gets a few respectable clients and is starting to really make some money and a name for himself. But then one day, one of his employees accidentally spills yellow paint all over a black Rolls Royce. After damages are assessed, you find that it's going to take about $18,000 to fix. While this is certainly unfortunate, being listed as a corporation ensures that it stops there, at the $18,000. It will never go beyond those assessed damages, no matter what. As a corporation, the owner of the Rolls cannot come back and take your house away.

2 - LONG LIFE, HAPPY LIFE

It should go without saying, but longevity is key to any business. It's such a simple concept that many miss the weight of it. It's especially crucial when you take into consideration that as of 2012, the average lifespan of a new business is just fifteen years. And, sometimes, it has nothing to do with the failure of the companies going under…it has to do with some other company coming along and doing what you can do better, faster, and in a new way.

If you happen to find yourself in this situation or if your company begins to show signs of going south, being listed as a corporation ensures that you will be around for quite some time.

When you have a corporation, you can essentially live forever. It never dies. Some of the biggest companies in America have been around for more than ninety years. Look at the Ford Motor Car Company. Henry Ford has been dead for over seventy years, and the company is still around and going strong. So not only is this a form of business immortality, but it is also quite conducive to growth.

3 - DON'T CHANGE THE RECIPE

The above reasons make the company a much more attractive purchase for potential buyers. A corporation is much easier to brand, and is also much easier for the public to connect with. This goes beyond simple public consumerism, though. It can also play a huge part in the selling of your company down the road.

If you have a business that is thriving, and has done so over a significant amount of time, you will likely have any number of potential buyers lined up to buy the name and the brand. This is advantageous to the potential buyer, because they are buying a proven brand. They do not want to start from scratch, struggling to make it out of the bottom.

This isn't just applicable to large businesses, either. Here's an example: there's a great Spanish restaurant just down the street from my office. It's been open for thirty years and has been owned and run by two different owners since I've been in my office since 2006. The original owners had no problem selling, because the restraint is well-known in the area. The new owners were not necessarily buying only a restaurant, they were buying a well-known name and the success that helped bolster it.

4 - INVEST IN THE PRESENT

This one sort of echoes back to the asset protection section above. Think about the big, impenetrable wall again. Even if you are a company that has racked up $35,000 in credit card debt and haven't paid it all off after your company goes under, the credit card companies can't come after your personal property or accounts.

That's not to say you should just freely run up credit card debt without being responsible, but as a company, it is great to have this security behind you.

Let me give you a real-life example. Let's say Jane has an up-and-coming dress shop. But things didn't quite pan out, and she had to close up shop after just eight months. But the lease they had signed for the building was for thirty-six months. Because Jane's company was a corporation, she's protected, regardless of the contract. The shopping center can only come after her company for the balance owed. Her personal assets are protected against the remaining months on her contract.

BUSINESS CARDS
An Oldie, but a Goodie

With social media, smartphones, and entire offices going completely digital, no one needs business cards anymore, right?

You'd think so, but you'd be wrong. But it is a mindset that seems to be creeping into the overall structure and approach of businesses. But as a general rule, it is good to continue to have business cards on you at all times. In today's modern and very electronic-based office settings, it may seem silly, but there is much more going on behind the exchange of business cards than meets the eye.

So, why continue to cling to this antiquated method of getting your name out there? Let me tell you a quick story.

Not too long ago, I crossed paths with a small business owner. He was a nice enough man, a hard-working guy who installed tile for a living. In our conversation, I learned that he was desperately seeking more business. When I asked him for his business card, he gave me one of those plain old boring Vista Print jobs. One-sided, flat, plain, and boring.

I asked him (being a bit of a hard-ass, maybe) if he had a million-dollar business. He laughed and said, "No." I explained to him that the road to a million-dollar business starts with good cards. I then broke down the math for him. He told me that his average project netted him around $1,000. I pointed out that good cards in the Miami area would run him around six cents a card, which comes out to $60 for one hundred nice, impressive cards. In other words, just one box of cards would only cost a small fraction of one of his jobs.

It's worth it, people. Something so small can say so much about your company and your personality. And here's why you need to take a serious stance on what so many people are incorrectly seeing as an antiquated tool.

1 - SIMPLE AND QUICK MARKETING

If you always have a business card in your wallet, pocket, briefcase, or portfolio, you are carrying around instant marketing. Let's say you're a house painter and run into some guy on the subway or at the airport. You strike up a conversation and find out that he's on the hunt for someone to paint his condo. Today's approach would require you to chatter off your number or website and hope the stranger will pull out his phone to type it all down.

But with a business card, you are physically handing him the information. More than that, you're handing him a representation of you and your company. You have just advertised your company without engaging in the awkward will they/won't they of hoping they will take your information down. Really, it's the best form of advertising you can get because really... who is going to flat out refuse a business card?

2 - KEEP YOURSELF IN SOMEONE'S POCKET

Business cards are shaped rather conveniently. They fit securely in your pocket, in most slots in wallets, and they make excellent book marks in a pinch. It wasn't too long ago (okay, who are we kidding, it's been a pretty good stretch ago) when multiple business cards could be found in just about any wallet or purse. While this is something that is seen less and less, it does still happen.

But even aside from wallets...take a look at an executive's office the next time you happen to be in one. Look on their desk or on their dry-erase or bulletin boards. Chances are you're going to see a few business cards. Sometimes, it might not even be because they are interested in the services on the cards; it's because they were given the card by a peer and hung onto it "just in case." This happens far more than you think… often enough to make it a smart decision to invest that tiny little bit of money into keeping a stack of business cards on hand.

3 - BECOME A FRIEND

When you hand someone a business card, there's a physical interaction. Even if two months pass until someone pulls out your card to contact you, there is a connection point between the two of you. They will remember meeting you. Even something as simple as "here's my card" is a great way to cement you into their minds. It's become an accepted way to advertise yourself without being spammy.

Anyone can hand out a business card. It doesn't take much talent or fortitude. But that's the beauty of it: not many people do it anymore. And you can use this to your advantage, because it will be even easier for the customer to remember your face, your company, and services.

Of course, it's not enough to simply have a business card. If you are going to stick to this old-school approach, you need to do it right. If you want to make sure you stand out in the form of a business card, here are some tips you need to consider.

Your business card should be a representation of your brand. Make sure the colors are uniform with other branding you are utilizing. If you have a logo (and you should!), make sure it is on the business card. This is essentially your first impression with a potential customer, so make sure it's a great one!

Use both sides of the card. Honestly, some might not even notice or pay attention to a blank second side. But they will pay attention if there is content on the second side as well. Not only does a double-sided business card just look better, it also offers you more space to convey more of your message, while also opening up the space and eliminating cluttered designs on the front.

Stay away from VistaPrint. Yes, they are widely known for their great deals and unbeatable prices. But they can offer those great deals because they skimp on product quality and don't offer the truly eye-catching details that other, more professional printers might be able to offer you. Any joker right off the street can go online and order up a plain old stack of 500 business cards for $9.99. You need to separate yourself from that. You need to keep that big company mindset in play in even small things like this and go the extra mile to make sure you stand out.

Make sure the information on your card is current. If you happen to move or get a new website, update your business cards right away. If it means eating two or three hundred old cards with your old information, that's just a cost you'll have to endure. What good is handing out dozens of business cards if the information is incorrect? It not only makes it harder for the customer to get in touch with you, but it looks unprofessional as well.

One bonus thought. The thicker your card is, the better.

VOICEMAIL
A Message Not Received is a Missed Customer

This is one of those areas where you might not think perception could come into play. After all, in a world driven by emails and texts, who leaves a voicemail message anymore?

The answer should be: "anyone who calls your number."

You want to give potential clients a reason to leave a message. You want to lead them to believe that if they don't leave a message for you to respond to, they could be missing out. This might take a bit of trickery on your part, but it's very easy to do. And, if this missed call just happens to be this customer's first impression of your company, you can make sure it's a very good one.

1 - KEEPING UP APPEARANCES

First of all, no matter how well-spoken you might be, you never want to have your own voice greeting a new customer. It may lead some to believe that you wear too many hats and that your company is relatively small. If possible, you should have the caller think that the voice they are hearing belongs to that of a secretary or receptionist. If you don't have someone with this sort of warm and inviting voice on staff, hire a professional voiceover artist to record it for you.

It might sound like a bit much, but you'd be surprised by how differently potential customers respond to this sort of voice asking them to leave a message rather than your own. Not only does it lead them to believe that you're far too busy to handle all the calls that come in, it also creates the perception that your company is rather large...large enough to need a receptionist and to not be able to field every single call that comes in.

2 - KEEP IT SCRIPTED

You want the caller to know that you do care about their call, but you also want them to know that you are a legitimately busy company. This can be achieved by sticking to a script that not only makes them feel valued and important, but establishes yourself as an important business, even before they have spoken to you.

There are obviously many ways you can go about doing this, but for the most part, a well-defined, yet brief voicemail greeting can accomplish it. The following example should be exactly what you need to get the point across:

"You have reached Awesome Company. We can't come to the phone right now, as we are busy helping other clients. But because your call is very important to us, if you leave a message with your name, number, and reason for your call, we will get back to you as soon as possible."

Stick to that or something very similar, and you're good to go.

Lastly, you should never simply say that you can't come to the phone. It sounds like a lazy excuse. To some, it may also sound as if you are far too busy. And if the caller thinks you are overworked and consistently busy, it might make them less open to working with you.

3 - BE AVAILABLE

See how the last part of that message above ends with you stating you will call them back? You have to always make good on that. If at all possible, return the call within a few hours. If you are legitimately too busy to engage in a lengthy call, at least make a courtesy call to explain to the caller that you received their message and would like to set aside some time when you are both free to speak at length.

You also want to make sure your mailbox is never full. This is just a deal-killer from every angle. First of all, it implies that you never check your messages. It makes the client think that even if they could leave a message, it would just get buried in the mounds of other messages you already have waiting. It also suggests that you are absolutely drowning—that you are so busy that you can't return voicemails, much less find fifteen minutes to speak to them.

All in all, the message on your voicemail recording presents more of a first impression than most people realize. It can be a great way to build upon your perception and to affect how others see you.

GOOGLE
How to Use the Most Powerful Tool on the Planet

The marketplace is filled with numerous choices—sometimes, too many choices. Ever since the first business went online, others have followed in its footsteps. Small businesses are now more than just the little bakery or tee-shirt shop down the block. Now, they exist in the form of websites and social media. Similarly, because of the Internet, phone books are a thing of the past. Google has essentially become the new version of the Yellow Pages, and it's very important that your name stands out among the rest.

For some, this may seem like a daunting fact if you are hoping to really define yourself in a way that will make you stand out in a very crowded digital age. But if you know the ins and outs of Google, it's much easier than you might think.

1 - GETTING A GOOGLE BUSINESS ACCOUNT

When you set your business up on Google, it's instrumental that you make it a business account. With a business account, you're offered many huge advantages that others miss out on, because they either didn't know about it or were too lazy to put a little extra work in. And really, when you're dealing with Google, they do all the work for you.

With a Google Business account, you essentially have built-in marketing. More than that, it's a public forum where customers and clients can leave reviews and feedback. If you can position yourself to be among the top Google search results in your industry or field, the power you wield is pretty much limitless. The number of new customers and exposure can literally change the way the world sees you. Plus, you get all of that attention and new business with Google doing most of the driving, allowing you to put forth more effort elsewhere.

2 - EASY ACCESS

When you have a Google Business Account, everything about your business is out there in one easy-to-find-place: your website, phone number, physical address, and even reviews. From that one, central location, clients both existing and new can contact you in many different ways. It makes things convenient not only for you, but for your clients, as well.

You'll quickly find how beneficial Google can be for your business if you set it all up with a watchful eye. However, you must be careful not to get too comfortable with Google and all of the many services it offers. As we are about to discuss, sometimes Google can make it a little too easy on us and without realizing it, we become passive and a little lazy.

3 - USING GOOGLE THE RIGHT WAY

When you get a Google account, you get a Gmail email address by default. This can be a handy tool, but it should not be the address you use for your email address. If you adore the Gmail setup, there are ways to have your professional business email linked to it, but you should never present your company email address as ending with "@gmail.com". It looks a little unprofessional and might give potential clients the impression that you weren't willing to drop a little money on your own domain name or email server.

Also, you need to know that Google is so well-known for a reason. Did you know that they also own YouTube? It's true. Speaking of which….

4 - USING VIDEOS

When you sign up for a Google account, you not only get all of the Google Business bells and whistles, but you also get access to your own YouTube account, which might be one of the most powerful tools available to you.

Quick...run a Google search on something right now. Anything. You'll notice right away that within the first two to three listings that come back to you, there's a YouTube video. You should take note of this, mainly because YouTube is the go-to for research these days—from learning how to get a stain out of a shirt to how to start a six-figure business from home.

What is your business? What is your niche? Whatever it is, you should be enough of an expert in it to create a video on that topic. Tell the public what you do and why you are the right person to be in that position. By creating a video, you create an aura of expertise and trust. Take this opportunity to educate the world not only on what you and your business do, but let them know how it can impact and change their lives.

Creating a video does more than improve the public's perception of you, though. It also gives you a great opportunity to promote your business. No matter what the video is about, you need to always end it with a soft and friendly call to action and letting the viewer know how they can get in touch with you.

Also, you can put the video on your website and link it in just about any social media platform. A video can be used as a modern-day business card if you know what you're doing. It creates a whole new avenue for potential customers to interact with you. And best of all, YouTube is incredibly user-friendly. You don't have to be tech-savvy to take advantage of it.

The simple matter is that if you want to be viewed as an expert in your field, you seriously need to look into making your own video— or even a series of videos. With this form of marketing, the sky is truly the limit.

EMAIL
Easy to Use, Easy to Abuse

Everyone has an email address, and some people are far too reliant on them. Upwards of 90 percent of communication between customers and clients take place in emails. Because of this, true professionals can no longer treat emails as nothing more than a quick and effective way to contact clients, family, and friends.

Even with something as simple as your email account, you can continue to shape public perception towards you and your company. Below, you'll find some valuable tips and tricks to help you do this, but first let's take a look at how a typical email interaction usually plays out.

Let's say you are emailing a potential client, following up from an initial conversation you recently had. You send off the mail after proofreading it and, then, wait for a response. Recent studies show that emails are typically responded to within four to six hours. So, let's say you get a response back within five. Your questions are answered in the response, and as far as you can tell, there's a chance the client will end up bringing business your way.

Seems good, right? Well, it is, but there were so many missed opportunities there, missed opportunities to help you stand out from your competition.

Yes, even in the structure and approach of your email.

1 - NO FREEBIES

Sure, we all want to cut costs wherever we can, but your email address is not one of those areas. In many cases, your email address is the first thing people really pay attention to, especially if they are trying to contact you online. With so many people out there competing for your business, something as small as a unique email address can help.

Stay away from free email services like Gmail or Yahoo. And if you still have an AOL or Hotmail account, kill that thing now and start all over. Nothing screams "unprofessional" like a business that still has people sending referrals and inquiries to an address ending in anything other than their business name. There are many different ways to acquire your own individualized email server, some of which cost less than $100 a year. Find the one that works best for you...the one that helps you stand out over the competition.

2 - KEEP IT SIMPLE

No matter what your business name is, keep your email address as simple as possible. If your name is Bob and you run a company called Everyday Marketing Solutions for You, you're going to be dealing with a nightmare if your email address is bob@everydaymarketingsolutionsforyou.com.

Shorten it any way you can. Use abbreviations, making it bob@emsforyou.com if you have to. But make sure your address is short, brief, and easy to remember. The more closely related to your business you can make it, the better.

3 - BELLS AND WHISTLES

People who have only a basic understanding of email know enough to send and receive messages. But if you own a business, you should really take the time to learn all of the different nooks and crannies hiding in the settings of your email service.

It is always a good idea to add a bit of flair to just about anything associated with your company. With emails, this can be done with a simple signature to go along with your mail. More often than not, this is simply a small graphic beneath your name, usually with a phone number or website URL included—anything to point them back to your business. It does not have to be fancy; it can just be your logo. It should not be too big or too small. Just about every email service worth its salt has this feature built-in, and can even tell you how big the image should be, as well as how to upload the image so that it automatically loads with each mail you send. Even a complete novice can have this done in less than five minutes.

You also need to make sure you understand how to use autoresponders. These are handy tools that allow you to set up automated responses to emails that come through when you are away. For instance, if you are planning a family vacation and know that you will be away and not able to answer emails for several days, an autoresponder can be sent to each person that sends you an email, stating that you are away for a few days and will return their mail when you get back. This way, they are expecting you to get back to them, rather than wondering if you even appreciate their interest at all.

Autoresponders are also great ways to follow up with clients. They can be sent several days after an initial correspondence, set to a timer and sent out automatically, rather than organically generated each and every time. It not only makes work easier on you, but helps to keep the lines of communication with that client open.

4 - BACK TO BASICS

Beyond all of these tips and tactics, you also need to remember that even emails are a representation of you and your business. Don't get chatty when communicating with clients in email conversations. Always keep it professional and on point. Even though it is an electronic communication, do not, under any circumstances, respond to clients with slang terms, abbreviations, or smiley faces.

Even in this detached form of communication, you always want to present your best self. Stay on point, address the topic of the mail efficiently and without rabbit trails. It is important to remember that every email you send is a reflection of you and your company, and even the slightest misstep can affect the way others might perceive you.

REMAINING RELEVANT
How to Stay in Front of Others in a Rapidly Evolving Digital World

About thirty years ago, the key to making it as a business involved building a strong list of contacts, pouring money into marketing and advertisements, and good old-fashioned pounding the pavement.

But a lot has changed in the last half century or so. Now, in order for your business to remain relevant and always in the mind of the public, you must think digitally. You can't have an archaic mindset when it comes to technology. You need to not only embrace it, but learn how to make it work for you.

1 - TAKE WHAT'S FREE

You can literally be found on Google without spending a penny. Of course, the more money you spend to make sure you are found, the better. But the Internet makes it simple for people to find you without much investment. And it comes down to much more than someone just typing your name or your company name into that Google search bar. As we discussed earlier, Google allows customers to leave feedback and ratings for other customers to see. But beyond that, there are other free listing tools you can use.

Yelp, for example, Yes, I know...some of you may not have heard of Yelp. But if that's the case, you need to learn about it as soon as possible. Any online platform that allows your customers to leave reviews and feedback needs to be utilized. And because these services are usually free, it is the most cost-effective way out there to spread the word about your business. Only...here's the great part: you aren't doing the spreading. It's other people— usually clients— that are spreading the word for you. And they are doing it 24/7 all around the world!

2 - THE OFTEN-CONFUSING WORLD OF SEARCH ENGINE OPTIMIZATION

If you want your business website to stand out, you're going to have to start to understand search engine optimization (also known as SEO). You can learn the basics of it on your own, but this is typically one area where you're going to have to shell out some money to get a pro to do it.

In a nutshell, SEO is the creation of keywords that are built into your website. These keywords, when used correctly and in the right combination, can ensure that your website will be among the first—if not *the* first—people will see when searching for certain terms that are relevant to your industry.

If you are running a commerce-based website, SEO can legitimately make or break you. SEO makes sure that search engines understand exactly what your website is about (and, similarly, what your business is all about), so that it knows to recommend you to the searcher. In other words, if you want to remain relevant in a highly competitive digital world, you need to make sure your SEO game is on point.

3 - TARGETING CUSTOMERS

This plays a bit into the SEO portion above, but to stay relevant in today's fast-paced business world, you must know how to target your customers. Fortunately, this is yet another area the Internet has made it very easy to succeed at. First, as we have already seen, there is SEO to consider.

But aside from that, there are numerous simple approaches you can take to make sure your message and content is reaching the people who actually want to hear it. Most of it starts with social media. For example, you can use your Twitter account to find people who show an interest in your industry. It's as simple as a few clicks, and, depending on your industry, you can find hundreds of potential clients. The same is true of Facebook as well, though shifting privacy issues on their platform makes it a bit harder.

One good way to look at it is this: if you have an important message about your business, would you rather scream your lungs out from a mountaintop, hoping a few interested parties would hear it, or would you rather stand at a podium, addressing a smaller crowd, though each member of that crowd is very interested in what your business can offer? You'll save yourself plenty of time and heartache if you narrow your focus down to those who are specifically interested in your industry. By targeting your customers in such a way, you eliminate much disappointment and empty work.

3 - ENGAGE, ENGAGE, ENGAGE

Let's say a potential customer has easily found your website, thanks to your high-profile videos and your great SEO work. But once they get there, looking for more information, they come across your latest entry to your site...and it's from three years ago. This will automatically raise a red flag, making that potential customer assume you're a little behind on the times. Keep this in mind not only as you promote your business vocally, but on social media as well. Share links and thoughts on current events within your industry. And every now and then, drop a link to some of your own content as well. This not only makes you stand out as an apparent expert in your field, but it also gives people the feeling that you are all about engaging with your audience. And when you feel personable to them, they are more likely to come to you with their business.

MANAGING YOUR VIRTUAL STOREFRONT
"Automated" Doesn't Mean You Get the Day Off

We've touched quite a bit on automation throughout this book and how it can be a massive asset to your business. After all, if the Internet is providing certain services for free, why not make use of them? The tricky part is to not become too reliant on a digital representation of yourself. You should never let your virtual storefront be the end-all be-all of your perception.

But before we get into the pitfalls of becoming too dependent on a virtual storefront, let's first make sure you understand what a virtual storefront is. It's one thing to have a website, but a totally different thing to have an effective virtual storefront. Your website needs to be a place where potential customers can get in touch with you about anything they have questions about.

This includes, but is not limited to:

- At least three ways to contact you (social media handles, phone number, email address).
- Videos to explain who you are and what you do.
- Customer reviews.
- A way for them to buy products that takes no more than one mouse-click.
- An "About Us" page.
- Colors and imagery that reflect your brand.

When someone visits your online presence, they should feel as though they are legitimately in a digital representation of your "store". Give them a consumer-based experience while also making them feel comfortable and not as though they are being bludgeoned with a sales pitch. A couple of ways to make sure you get the most out of your virtual storefront are found below, but don't be afraid to customize and think outside of the box from time to time.

1 - ACCESSIBILITY

Like any good store, the customer should be able to easily locate what they are looking for. Be sure your storefront and/

or website is simple to navigate. Did you know that a 2017 study shows that the typical person will only spend about eight seconds on any given website if what they are looking for is not easily accessible?

This can usually be achieved by using easy-to-read menu bars or drop-down menus. Whatever you choose to do, make sure your site is user friendly, free of clutter, and simple to use.

2 – ONE-STOP SHOPPING

In today's business world, it's not enough to be able to provide a business number and a cell number. People expect to be able to reach out to you on any number of social media platforms, the three biggest being Facebook, Twitter, and Instagram. Because of this, you should have easy-to-find links on your site, usually in the form of badges or icons.

You also want to give customers easy access to your email. Sometimes, you might find it helpful to have multiple email addresses for them to choose from. This not only gives them more options, but it makes your company look bigger, too. Consider having an email address for "support", "info", or "queries".

3 - SHIPPING

If your business sells physical goods that will be shipped in the mail, you want to look very professional in this area, too. Because of that, I suggest using the UPS store for every shipping need. It's not only a more secure option than mailing things off like normal at the post office, but it gives the customer a more secure feeling as well.

It's one of those things we never really think about until we receive a package. Are you going to think better of a company if your item is delivered in a folded and wrinkly USPS package or in a nice, firm, and well-taken-care-of UPS package? This is one of the many areas where it helps to stand in the customer's shoes and to try to see things from their perspective.

4 - KNOW WHERE TO DRAW THE LINE

While it is perfectly fine to offer customers and potential customers access to your social media platforms and email addresses, don't take it any farther than that. You should not under any circumstances allow anyone who comes to your virtual storefront your home address. Some people even hesitate to supply their personal cell number, but this really just comes down to personal preference.

When it comes to addresses, though, you want to make sure you do have a reliable physical address. But as we have just discussed, it should not be your home address. If you work from home and not out of an office, this can be resolved by renting a post-office box from the post office. To be honest, in today's digital world, you may not even use the physical address all that much, but it is simply one more thing you can use to your advantage when it comes to how people perceive you and your business.

5 - LOOK PROFESSIONAL

This should go without saying, but in everything you do, you need to make sure you look professional. Most of the time, this simply means not making any careless mistakes. Let me give you an example.

Let's say your site is up and running and it looks great! You're so excited. But after a few days, you start to realize that you aren't getting any emails. You get a few calls here and there, but no emails. You sit down and look over your site, making sure the linked email address is easy to find. And while you discover that it is, indeed, simple to find, there is still an error: the email address you inserted into the site is wrong. You've misspelled your own business name.

This is not only unprofessional and sloppy, but it likely resulted in you missing several emails about potential sales or jobs.

These sorts of things happen all the time. This is why you need to have someone other than yourself look over each and every word that goes onto your digital storefront. This is one of the reasons I suggested using a short email address earlier in this book. It eliminates the chance of mistakes...not only on your end, but on the end of any customer trying to get in touch with you as well.

A few other small things you can do that add to upping your perception are:

Try to get you name or business name on everything. Your URL, your email address, even your social media handles.

As an example, let's say you just opened up a pizza parlor called Buzz Pizza. Your email address should be something like info@buzzpizza.com. Your Twitter handle should be @buzzpizza, and so on.

It's been stated before, but needs to be stressed again. Your email address should NEVER end with "aol", "gmail", or "yahoo". It screams amateur.

Make sure your website is mobile friendly. There are some people who use their phones for nearly all of their online communications these days. If your site is not mobile friendly, it will look ugly and off-center on phones and some tablets.

Offer a newsletter option for your clients. Set aside some time each week to come up with interesting content regarding your industry, or even just share some links to news articles related to your business. Keeping an open line of communication with your customers outside of basic social media exchanges can go a long way and keep you fresh in their minds.

STORIES OF PERCEPTION

I told you at the beginning of this book that I started out from nothing. I wasn't exaggerating. I was not born into wealth, and I never had anything handed to me, with the exception of a meager job cleaning hotel rooms for my family.

Today, I own my own accounting business and average a thousand returns a year. I work hard and have followed the principles in this book for decades. This dedication and hard work has made it possible for me to work just ninety-six days a year.

I wrote this book for you because of errors in thinking I see up-and-comers making on a daily basis. I travel around the world to conferences and seminars, not only to share what I have learned, but to keep learning from others.

I met a man recently in the airport in Las Vegas. His story shows how close you can get and still miss the prize.

We were waiting to board our plane, and we started to strike up conversation, nothing serious at all, just passing conversation in an airport. He was going to a hardware show, and even though I am not particularly interested in that industry, I still asked for his business card, because it never hurts to make a connection.

He handed me his card, and I noticed right away that it was a cheap and generic Vistaprint card. I immediately perceived this man's business as second-rate and less than excellent. I saw him as a man afraid to invest in his business. If a man is afraid to invest in his business, well, what does that say about the business?

I can promise you every one of his potential new customers thinks that way. My meeting with this man is a key example of why I wrote this book. Small mistakes like that can make or break your business. What people perceive about you will determine your success or destroy you.

I asked this man why he chose to use such an inexpensive card. His answer was, "Well, no one uses them anymore."

This was a ridiculous answer, because he was handing me one in that very moment! Here he was, about to go to a convention. Do you know the number one thing people exchange with one another at conventions and trade shows? That's right. Business cards.

He was making the incorrect assumption that no one would hold onto his card, and that it didn't matter. I can point to my wife to prove him wrong. My wife works in an office and holds on to every business card she gets. She does this so we will have a point of reference whenever we might need something. I guarantee you if we had a leak in our plumbing tonight, she'd have at least two business cards for local plumbers. She will call the one that speaks to her the loudest.

See how close he was getting to being the best at success? He was heading to a show in order to make connections and hopefully grow his business. A lot of people don't understand the importance of attending things like conferences and events. It's about more than networking. It's about getting your name out there and learning about all of the new ways people within your industry are working. It's about getting in front of trends and making sure you are on the cutting edge of how your industry is shifting, changing, and evolving. But he was going to be less than successful because of his failure to make a lasting impression with something as simple a business card.

A few years ago, I went to a conference out west. I learned a few things and met a few people, and it was, all in all, a good experience. There is one thing that still stands out to me. It was meeting a fellow named Tim, a man who recommended that I attend another event I had never heard of. I made the decision to go. Once there, I met Manny, who taught me all about Facebook marketing, the single most important tool I now use that drives my success, enabling me to reach thousands of people for my business.

All because I met Tim at the event out west.

By constantly showing up at events connected with your lifework, you create new and expanding opportunities for yourself to evolve your perception. When you attend conferences and events, people will start to recognize your name and face. If you're doing it right, people will start to look forward to seeing you at these events. And if you're *really* doing it right, people will want to hear you talk at these events. People will start to think of you as an expert in your field.

At that level, you have truly started to master the art of perception.

I want the very best for you. I want you to be the best at your success. If you see me somewhere, stop and say hello. But you are warned.

I am a hugger.

About The Author

Albert Corey

Author - Speaker - Tax Strategist

For more than thirty years, Albert has been helping entrepreneurs, business owners and individuals the world over become the best at their success. Oh yes. He has an unconventional accounting practice in south Florida and makes more money than many of his neighbors. You can find him at ThePerceptionSystem.com.

Author Albert Corey with Grant Cardone

Author Albert Corey with Tony Robbins

www.ingramcontent.com/pod-product-compliance
Lightning Source LLC
LaVergne TN
LVHW021333080526
838202LV00003B/159